ALL ABOUT
BABY NAMES
NAMES FOR YOUR BABY

GP

GOO̶̶̶̶̶̶̶̶̶̶̶̶̶̶̶̶̶̶̶̶HOUSE™

B̶̶̶̶̶̶̶̶̶̶̶̶̶̶̶̶lace,

TEL.: 257508̶̶̶̶̶̶̶̶̶̶̶̶̶̶̶̶̶̶̶: 91-11-25763428

ALL ABOUT
BABY NAMES
NAMES FOR YOUR BABY

ISBN : 81-7245-355-8

Published by :

Rajneesh Chowdhry

GOODWILL PUBLISHING HOUSE™

B-3, Rattan Jyoti, 18 Rajendra Place,
NEW DELHI-110 008 (INDIA)
TEL.: 25750801, 25755519, 25820556 FAX : 91-11-25763428
E-Mail: goodwillpub@vsnl.net
Website: www.goodwillpublishinghouse.com

Printed at: Kumar Offset, Delhi.

Publisher's Note

The world is so large and mysterious that it is almost impossible to study each and every subject and identify the reason and logic beholding it. 'All About' is a series of illustrated books, designed to create awareness about such few subjects. The topics and subjects are related with your daily life, which have amazed us at times.

The series consists of books such as Feng Shui and Vaastu Shastra, which demonstrate the significance of directions in your life and the placement of objects, and house setting, from the Chinese and Indian perspective.

People with an inclination towards fortune telling have a lot to choose from, as the collection comprises of books ranging from Palmistry to Astrology to Numerology. Moreover, you can also analyse your Love and Star Signs.

All the health conscious people can get some handy health tips to keep fit. Moreover, the reader can learn about Yoga, to keep in shape. A few tips on Relaxation, Chakras, Tantric Sex, Reiki and Sex for Healing can provide you with helpful guidelines on how to relax after the day's work.

You can also learn all about the diseases that have enveloped the human race. The series provides all information on Diabetes, Diarrhoea, Constipation, Heart Attack, Kidney Stones, Anxiety, Typhoid, Hepatitis, Headache etc.

The series also mentions some of the most amazing and mystifying topics like Hypnosis, Face Reading, Body language and Magnetotherapy. To have a good tinkling experience the readers can enjoy some of the funniest jokes in the Joke Book. Further, you can also mobilize your brain cells in the book on Riddles.

Overall, 'All About' is an immense pool of information and facts that have always amused the living beings. It is an accumulation of the diverse, mysterious, realistic, day-to-day issues you always wanted to know about.

Contents

1. Baby Names Boys   7

2. Baby Names Girls   82

Introduction

Every body in this world bears a name. The name is an identity of a person. Name is something that differentiates a person from another. It gives an individuality to a person. The name also reflects the personality, the religion and also tells about the person's antecedents. In India, the ceremony of name keeping is called 'Namkaran', where a priest helps in keeping the name that are usually adopted from the religious books. But in the changing times, people prefer to call the child as per their liking.

A name usually has two parts. The first name is the identity of the person whereas the second name tells about the parents or the village of a person. This is a collection of few names that may assist you in naming your child.

Baby Names Boys

A

Aaditya	Sun
Aakaar	Shape
Aakash	Sky
Aarav	Peaceful
Aarit	One who seeks the right direction
Aariz	Respectable man; Intelligent
Aaron	Enlightened; To Sing
Aarpit	To donate
Aarth	Meaning
Aarush	First ray of sun
Aashish	Blessing
Aatish	Fireworks; Name of Lord Ganesha
Abbott	Father
Abe	Father of a Multitude
Abel	A breath
Abhay	Fearless

Abheek	Fearless
Abhi	Fearless
Abhijay	Victor
Abhijeet	Victorious; One who has been/has conquered
Abhilash	Wish; Desire
Abhim	Vishnu
Abhinav	An act
Abhinay	Expression
Abhineet	Perfect
Abhinivesh	Desire
Abhiraj	Fearless King
Abhiram	Joyous
Abhiru	Shiva
Abhishek	Ritual
Abhiyasana	Vishnu
Abhur	Vishnu
Abie	God is Joy
Abimanyu	Arjuna's son
Abjinipati	Surya
Adeep	Light
Adhidar	Lord Krishna
Adimurti	Lord Vishnu
Adinath	Lord Vishnu
Adishankara	Lord Shiva

Adithya	Sun God; Son of Adithi
Aditya	Sun
Advait	Unique
Advaita	Focussed
Advay	Unique
Agampreet	Love for God
Ajayoni	Lord Shiva
Ajit	Victorious
Ajitabh	Victor
Ajitesh	Lord Vishnu
Ajmil	A mythological king
Ajoy	Joyful
Akaldeep	God's lamp
Akalpreet	Love of God
Akand	Calm
Akarsh	Attractive
Akash	Sky
Akhil	Complete
Aksaj	Lord Vishnu
Aksal	Lord Shiva
Akshar	Letter
Akshat	Rice used in worship
Akshay	Immortal
Akshit	Permanent

Amitava	One with boundless; Splendour
Amitesh	Limitless
Amod	Pleasurable
Amogh	Lord Ganesh
Amol	Priceless
Amolik	Priceless
Amresh	Lord Indra
Amrish	Lord Indra
Amrit	Nectar
Amshu	Atom
Amshul	Bright
Amulya	Invaluable; Princess
Anadi	Eternal
Anant	Joyful; Unending
Aneesh	Supreme
Anek	Many
Angad	Mythological name
Angaj	Son
Anik	Soldier
Anikait	Lord of the world
Aniketh	Lord of all
Anil	God of wind
Animesh	Bright
Aniruddh	Grandson of Lord Krishna

Anirvan	Undying
Anish	Lord Vishnu
Anit	Joyful; Unending
Anjal	Hollow formed by joining two hands
Anjana	Dusky
Anjas	Fortright
Arjit	Earned
Arjun	Lord Krishna's cousin
Arpan	Offering
Arun	Sun
Arvind	Lotus
Aryaman	Noble-minded; Aristocratic; Sun
Ashirvad	Blessing
Ashish	Blessing
Ashutosh	A name of Lord Shiva
Ashvath	Strong
Ashwath	Banyan tree
Ashwin	A star
Asutosh	One who becomes happy easily
Atal	Unshakeable
Atambhu	The Holy trinity
Atamveer	Brave
Atharva	Name of Lord Ganesha; The first Vedas

Atin	The great one
Atmanand	Blissful
Avilash	Faithful
Avinash	Immortal; Inconquerable
Avkash	Leisure
Avtar	Holy incarnation
Ayavanth	Lord Shiva
Ayush	Age; Duration of life

B

Bahurup	Lord Brahma
Bajrang	Lord Hanumanji
Bakul	Lord Shiva
Balachandar	Young moon
Baladuish	Lord Indra
Balahant	Lord Indra
Balaji	Lord Venkatesh
Balanuj	Lord Krishna
Balashvar	Lord Krishna
Barindra	The Ocean
Bart	Son of Tolmai
Bartholemew	Hill; Furrow
Barton	Barley farm
Baruch	Blessed

Barun	Lord of the sea
Bary	Marksman
Base	The Short One
Bash	Forerunner
Bastien	Venerable; Revered
Bat	Short for Bartholomew
Baxter	A baker
Bayard	With red-brown hair
Bayle	Beautiful
Baylee	Bailiff
Bhabru	Lord Vishnu
Bhagirath	A pious king
Bhagyaraj	Lord of faith
Bhairav	Lord Shiva
Bharat	Lord Rama's brother
Bharddwaj	A sage
Bhargav	Lord Shiva
Bhargavan	Name of deity in Ahobilam (AP)
Bhargavi	Goddess Durga; Laxmi; Parvati; Daughter of Sun
Bhartesh	King of Bharat
Bishanpal	Raised by God
Brahamjeet	God's triumph
Brent	Hill top
Brijesh	Lord Krishna

C

Cache	Storage place
Cade	Pure
Caden	Fighter
Cael	Victorious people
Caolan	Form of Helen
Capricorn	The goat
Chaitanya	A famous sage
Chakradev	Lord Vishnu
Chakradhar	Lord Vishnu
Chakravarthi	King
Chanakya	Bright
Chandran	Moon
Chandrashekar	Lord Shiva
Chandresh	Lord Shiva; Moon
Charan	Feet
Chatresh	Lord Shiva
Chhatrabhuj	Lord Vishnu
Chinmay	Supreme consciousness; Name of Lord Ganesha
Chiranjiv	Immortal
Chitesh hatma	Big Soul
Chunmay	Supreme Consciousness

D

Dacey	Down below
Dacian	From Dacia (Near Rome)
Dafydd	Beloved
Dagan	Grain of corn
Dasharathi	Lord Rama
Dayaram	Merciful
Deepinder	God's light
Devendra	Lord Indra
Devjeet	God's triumph
Devkumar	Son of God
Dhananjay	Arjuna
Dhanesh	Lord of wealth
Dhanraj	King of wealth
Dharamdeep	Lamp of religion
Dharamdev	God of faith
Dhiraj	Patience
Dhruv	Firm
Digvijay	Conqueror
Divjot	Divine light

E

Eadoin	Blessed with many friends
Eamon	Wealthy protector
Earnest	Truth
Eben	Rock
Echo	Sound returned
Ed	Wealthy guardian
Edan	Full of fire
Eddie	Wealthy guardian
Eddy	Protector
Eden	Paradise
Ekansh	Whole
Ekantin	Lord Vishnu
Ekapad	Lord Shiva
Ekaraj	Emperor
Ekavir	Bravest of the brave
Ekavira	Lord Shiva's daughter
Eklavya	The student who learned bow by watching
Ekram	Honour
Elam	Highlands
Elan	Tree
Elden	Protector

Eldon	Of old age
Eleazar	God has helped
Elisha	God is gracious
Eljah	Form of Elijah
Elkan	Belonging to God
Ellard	Nobly brave
Ellery	Elder tree island
Elliot	The Lord is my God
Evyavan	Lord Vishnu

G

Gabe	From the name Gabriel
Gabriel	Hero of the God
Gad	Juniper tree
Gael	Gaelic; From Ireland
Gaerwn	White fort
Gaetan	From Gaeta, Italy
Gaetano	Region in Italy
Gagan	Sky
Gautam	Lord Buddha
Ghanshyam	Lord Krishna
Girdhari	Lord Krishna
Girindra	Lord Shiva
Giriraj	God of the mountains

Gopal	Lord Krishna
Gopati	Lord Vishnu
Gopesh	Lord Krishna
Govinda	Lord Krishna
Gunvant	Virtuous
Gurjas	Fame of lord
Gurman	Heart of guru
Gurudankar	Lord Vishnu
Gurudeep	Lamp of the guru
Gurveer	Warrior of the guru
Gurvinder	Guru

H

Haben	Pride
Habib	Beloved one
Hadar	Glorious
Hadley	Heath near the wasteland
Hagen	Not available
Hagop	Supplanter
Haig	Legend; From the Field
Haines	From a vined cottage
Hajari	Flight
Hakan	Fire

Hakesh	Lord of sound
Hardy	Courageous; Strong
Harekrishna	Lord Krishna
Harendra	Lord Shiva
Hariaksa	Lord Shiva
Harindra	A tree
Harish	Lord Shiva; Lord Krishna
Harlan	From the army
Harley	Spacious meadow
Harlow	Troops on the hill
Harmendra	Moon
Harmon	Soldier
Harold	Army ruler
Haroun	Lofty
Harper	Harp player
Harris	Son of Harry
Heaton	High ground
Hector	Anchor; Steadfast
Heinz	Household ruler
Helki	Touch
Hem	Gold; Lord Buddha
Hitendra	Well wisher
Hitesh	Lord of goodness
Hrishikesh	Lord Vishnu

I

Iago	Supplanter
Iain	God is gracious
Ife	Wide; Love
Indra	God of the skies
Indrajit	Victor over Indra
Indranuj	Lord Vishnu
Indravaraj	Lord Vishnu
Indravishnu	Lord Indra
Indumal	Lord Shiva
Inesh	Lord Vishnu
Infinity	Endless
Ingo	Male leader
Inigo	Ardent
Ion	God is good
Ira	Watchful; Descendant
Iram	Shining
Iravan	King of ocean
Iravat	Rain clouds
Ireland	Homage to Ireland
Irish	From Ireland
Irm	Surya; Always on the move; Nature liked

Irving	Handsome and fair
Isaiah	Salvation by God
Ish	Lord Vishnu
Ishir	Agni; Strong; Efficient; Agile
Ishmael	God will hear
Ismael	God will hear
Ismail	God will hear
Ismet	Honour
Isra	Freedom
Israel	Prince of God
Issay	Hairy
Ivan	God is good
Ivo	Cut wood
Ivrit	The Hebrew language
Izzy	He will laugh

J

Jabari	Fearless
Jabilo	Medicine man
Jabir	Comforter
Jabulani	Happy
Jace	Moon-Var. of Jacey
Jacey	From the initials J.C.

Jacie	Variation of Jace
Jack	From the name John
Jackson	Son of Jack
Jacob	Supplanter
Jacques	From the name Jacob
Jada	Wise
Jade	Green gemstone
Jaden	God has heard
Jadon	He will judge
Jaegar	Hunger
Jaeger	Hunter
Jafari	Dignified
Jafaru	Brook; Creek
Jag	The universe
Jagesh	Lord of the universe
Jagger	To carry
Jagish	Lord of the universe
Jagmohan	Lord Krishna
Jaguar	Large spotted feline
Jai	Lord Shiva
Jaideep	Victory to the light
Jaidev	Lord of victors
Jaigopal	Victorious Lord Krishna
Jamil	Handsome
Jamison	James' son

Janak	Lord Buddha; Father of Sita
Janesh	Lord of men
Japesh	Lord Shiva
Jaswant	Victorious
Jatin	Lord Shiva
Jayant	Lord Shiva
Jayendra	Lord of victory
Jayesh	Victor
Jayin	Conqueror
Jigar	Heart
Jignesh	Intellectual curiosity
Jina	Lord Vishnu
Jinadev	Lord of victory
Jinendra	Lord of victory
Jinesh	Jain God's name
Jitendra	One who can conquer Indra
Jogesh	Lord Shiva
Joginder	Lord Shiva
Jograj	Lord Shiva
Joideep	Light of happiness

K

Kaalanjay	Lord Krishna

Kadeem	Servant
Kaden	Fighter
Kadin	Companion
Kael	Mighty warrior
Kaelem	Honest
Kaelin	Rejoicer; Waterfall pool
Kaemon	Joyful
Kai	Ocean
Kaikura	Ground squirrel
Kail	Mighty one
Kailas	Home of the Lord
Kailash	Abode of Lord Shiva
Kaili	Hawaiian God
Kaipo	Sweetheart
Kaiser	Leader
Kalani	The heavens
Kalap	Moon
Kalb	Faithful; Bold
Kale	Man
Kaleb	From Caleb-Faithful; Bold
Kalei	One who works for the King
Kamlesh	The preserver; Lord Vishnu

Kamran	Successful
Kapila	Prophet
Kapish	Lord Hanuman
Kapono	Righteous
Karan	Pure
Karan	Instrument
Kare	Enormous
Kareem	Very generous
Karif	Arrived in autumn
Karik	Form of Carrick
Karim	From the name Kareem
Karimah	Generous one
Kasish	Lord Shiva
Kaspar	From the name Casper
Kass	Blackbird
Kateb	Writer
Kato	Good judgement
Katungi	Rich
Kaushal	Wealth
Kaushik	A wise sage
Kautik	Joy
Kavel	Lotus
Kavi	Poet
Kaycee	Initals K and C

Kayo	From Initials K.O.
Kedar	Lord Shiva
Keerthinath	Famous person
Keshat	Lord Vishnu
Keshav	Lord Krishna
Keshto	Lord Hanuman
Ketak	Flower
Ketan	Home; Banner
Ketu	Lord Shiva
Ketubh	Cloud
Khushal	Happy
Kingshuk	A bright red flower
Kinshuk	Nice
Kirat	Lord Shiva
Kiratidev	Lord of light
Kireeti	Another name for Arjun
Kirit	Crown
Kirtan	A form of worship
Kirti	Fame
Kirtin	Celebrated
Kishan	Lord Krishna
Kishlaya	Lotus; Fresh leave
Kishor	The Sun God
Kishore	Lord Krishna

Kiyedh	Lord Indra
Koundinya	Sage
Kovidh	Wise
Kripal	Compassionate
Kshitij	Lord of Earth
Kshrugal	A name of God Shiva
Kuber	God of wealth
Kuldeep	Light of the house
Kuvar	Fragrance

L

Laban	White
Lachlan	From the lake
Laddie	Attendant
Laird	Head of the household
Lajos	Famous holy man
Laken	From the lake
Landry	Rough land
Lane	Narrow road
Lang	Tall one
Langer	Tall man
Langston	Town of the giant
Lani	Sky

Laurence	Laurel-Crowned
Laurent	Crowned with laurel
Lave	Burning rock
Lavender	A purple flowering plant
Lavey	From the name LeviI
Lavi	Lion
Lavitra	Lord Shiva
Lawrence	Laurel-crowned
Lawson	Son of Lawrence
Laxman	Lord Rama's brother
Layne	Narrow road
Lekh	Document
Liladhar	Lord Vishnu
Lohendra	Lord of three worlds
Lohitaksh	Lord Vishnu
Lokesh	Lord Brahama
Loknath	Lord Vishnu
Lukesh	King of the empire
Luv	Lord Rama's twin son

M

Maalolan	Name of deity in Ahobilam(AP)
Maan	Mind

Maeron	Bitter
Maeryn	Bitter
Maharanth	Pollen inside a flower
Mahari	Forgiver
Maharvan	Lord Shiva
Mahatru	Lord Vishnu
Mahavir	Lord Hanuman
Mahdi	The expected one
Mahendra	Lord Vishnu
Mahesh	Lord Shiva
Mahira	Lord Indra
Mahon	Bear
Maik	Now
Maimun	Lucky
Maine	Mainland
Maitland	Meadow
Maj	A pearl
Majed	Praise
Major	Better
Makaio	Gift of the God
Mangal	Auspicious
Mangesh	Lord Shiva
Manhar	Lord Krishna
Mani	Gem

Manish	Lord of the mind
Manit	Highly respected
Manmohan	Lord Krishna
Manobhu	Kama
Manoj	Mental love
Manthan	Reflection through study
Mardav	Simple
Marmit	Lord Shiva
Martand	Sun
Marudeva	Lord of the desert
Maruti	Lord Hanuman
Matheysh	Lord Shiva
Mayank	Moon
Mayur	Peacock
Meera	Lord Krishna's devotee
Meghaj	Pearl
Meghraj	King of clouds
Mehul	Rain
Mihir	Sun rays
Mikel	Who is like God?
Miller	Mill worker
Mills	Near the mills
Milo	From the name Miles
Milt	From the Mill Town

Milton	From the Mill Town
Mimir	God of prophecy
Ming yue	Bright moon
Mingan	Grey wolf
Minh	Bright and clever
Minor	Junior; Younger
Mio	Mine
Miracle	Divine act
Mirit	Bitter
Miroslav	Peace celebration
Misae	White hot sun
Misha	From the name Michael
Misu	Ripples in the water
Mitch	Who is like God?
Mitchell	Who is like God?
Miten	Male friend
Mitesh	A person with few desires
Mithun	A pair
Mitrajit	Friendly
Mitsu	Light
Mittul	Measured
Mitul	Friend
Mizell	Tiny gnat
Mo	Dark skinned

Moe	Dark skinned
Moeshe	Drawn out of the water
Mohan	Attractive
Mohan	Lovable; Lord Krishna
Mohawk	Native American tribe name
Mohit	Charming
Mohnish	Lord Krishna
Moke	Form of Moses
Molimo	Bear walking into the shade
Monahan	Religious man
Monet	Solitary
Monroe	Near the river Roe
Montague	Sharp cliff
Montana	Mountain
Montego	Mountainous
Montenegro	Black mountain
Montgomery	Of the mountain
Moon	From the moon
Moon-unit	One that orbits the moon
Moral	Lovely thoughts
Morathi	Wise man
Mordecai	Warrior; Warlike
More	Great

Morey	From the name Morris
Morgan	The edge of the sea
Morley	Of the Moor
Morpheus	God of dreams
Morrie	Moor
Morrigan	War Goddess
Morris	Dark skinned
Morrison	Son of Morris
Morse	Of the moors
Mort	Moor
Mortimer	Still water
Morty	From the name Mortimer
Moses	Drawn out of the water
Moshe	From the name Moses
Moss	From the water
Mostyn	Fortress in a field
Moti	Pearl
Mranalini	A collection of lotus
Mrigaj	Son of the moon
Mrigank	Moon
Mrigayu	Lord Shiva
Mrigyasa	Lord Shiva
Mrinal	Lotus
Mudit	Happy

Muhammad	Praised
Muhir	Lord Shiva
Mukesh	Lord Shiva; Lord of joy
Mukesh	Lord Shiva; Lord of joy
Mukul	Soul
Mukund	Lord Krishna
Muni	Village God
Munish	Lord Buddha
Muralidhar	Lord Krishna
Murari	Lord Krishna
Murugan	Tamil God

N

Naal	Birth
Naami	Lord Vishnu
Nabhasya	Lord Shiva; Belonging to the sky
Nabhendu	New moon
Nabhij	Lord Brahma; Born of a navel
Nabhya	Lord Shiva
Nabya	Lord Shiva
Nagendra	Lord Shiva
Nagesh	Lord Shiva

Nageshwaran	Lord Snake
Naiara	Of the Virgin Mary
Naif	Not available
Naiser	Founder of clans
Nakul	Lord Shiva
Nalagriv	Lord Shiva; One with a blue neck
Nalani	Heaven's calm
Nalesh	King of flowers
Nalin	Lotus flower
Nalin	Lotus
Nalo	Lovable
Nam	South or manly
Naman	Renowned; Namaskar
Namdev	Lord Vishnu
Namir	Swift cat
Namish	Lord Vishnu
Nandish	Lord of pleasure
Nansen	Son of Nancy
Nantai	Chief
Naparajit	Lord Shiva; Stubborn
Napoleon	Fierce one from Naples
Narayan	Lord Vishnu
Narayanan	Title of the Lord Vishnu
Nardo	From the name Bernard

Narendra	King of man
Naresh	King
Naresh	King
Narottam	Lord Vishnu
Nash	Adventurer
Nasser	Triumphant
Nat	Gift of the God
Nataraj	Lord Shiva
Nate	Gift of the God
Natesh	Lord Shiva
Nathan	Gift of the God
Nathan	Lord Krishna
Nathaniel	Gift of the God
Natine	Of the Natine tribe
Natividad	Of the nativity
Natsu	Born in summer
Nature	Nature
Natwar	Lord Krishna
Navarro	Plains
Navashen	The one who brings hope
Naveen	Beautiful; Pleasant
Naveen	New
Navid	Beloved

Navrang	Colourful
Nay	Highness and grace
Nayakan	Hero
Nayan	Eye
Nayef	Highness and grace
Neal	A champion
Neely	Victor
Neeraj	Lotus
Neil	Champion
Neka	Wild goose
Nelson	Son of Neal
Nemesio	Nemesis; God of vengeance
Nen	Ancient waters
Neo	New
Nero	Powerful
Neron	Strong
Nestor	Traveller
Nevada	Covered in snow
Nevan	Little saint
Neville	New town
Nevin	Nephew
Newlyn	From the spring
Newman	New comer
Newton	New town

Niabi	Fawn
Niall	Champion
Niamh	Bright
Nibal	Arrows
Nibaw	Standing tall
Nibodh	Wisdom
Nicholai	Victorious people
Nicholas	Victorious people
Nikash	Horizon
Niket	Home
Nikhil	Complete; Whole; Entire
Nikunj	Loving home; Lord Krishna
Nilabh	Moon
Nilesh	The dark Lord; Lord Krishna
Nimish	Lord Vishnu; The twinkling of an eye
Nimish	Momentary
Nipun	Proficient; Skillful; Clever
Niraj	Lotus
Niranjan	Lord Shiva
Nirbhay	Fearless
Nirgranth	Simple behaviour
Nirlep	Lord Shiva; Lord of dancers
Nirmal	Clean

Nirmay	Pure
Nirmit	Created
Nischal	Calm
Nishanth	Peaceful; Dawn
Nishesh	Moon
Nishith	Night
Nishkarsh	Result
Nishreyasal	Lord Shiva; The best
Nitin	New
Nitish	Lord Krishna's name
Nityanta	Lord Vishnu
Nridev	King amongst men
Nripesh	Lord of kings

O

Oakes	Beside the oak trees
Oakley	Field of oak trees
Obalesh	Lord Shiva
Obban	Lord Shiva
Obedience	To obey
Oberon	Bear heart
Obert	Wealthy
Octavio	The eighth

Octavious	Eighth
Octavius	The eighth
Odakota	Friend
Oded	Strong
Odell	Otter
Odin	Supreme God
Odysseus	Full of wrath
Ogden	From the valley of oaks
Ohanzee	Shadow
Ohio	Large river
Oistin	Venerable
Ojayit	Courageous
Okal	To cross
Okapi	Animal with long neck
Oke	Form of Oscar
Okoth	Born when it was Raining
Olaf	Ancestor
Oleg	Sacred
Olin	Of the ancestors
Oliver	Olive tree; Peace
Ollie	From the name Oliver
Om	Primordial sound
Oma	Commander
Omar	Ultimate devotee

Omega	Last
Omesh	Lord of the Om
Omeshwar	Lord of the Om
Omkar	Religious word Om
Omkarnath	Lord Shiva
Omprakash	Sacred light
On	Peace
Onan	Wealthy
Onofre	Defender of peace
Onslow	Hill of the passionate one
Oral	Speaker; Word
Oran	Green
Orane	Rising
Orde	Beginning
Ordell	Beginning
Oren	A tree
Orestes	Mountain man
Oriel	Gold
Orien	The Orient; East
Oringo	He who likes the hunt
Oriole	Golden; A gold beaked bird
Orion	A hunter in Greek mythology
Orlando	Land of the gold
Orleans	Golden

Orly	Light
Ormand	Serpent
Ornice	Cedar Tree
Oro	Gold
Orrick	Venerable oak
Orrin	River
Orsen	From the name Orson
Orsin	Bear
Orson	A bear
Orville	Golden city
Osama	Lion-like
Osborn	The bear of God
Oscar	Accurate spearsman
Osgood	God of the Heavens
Osias	Salvation
Osman	Tender youth
Osmond	Godly protector
Osric	Divine ruler
Ossie	God's divine power
Oswald	God of the forest
Othello	Prosperous
Otieno	Born at night
Otis	One who hears well
Otto	Wealthy
Overton	The upper town

Ovid	Egg shaped
Ovidio	Shepherd
Owen	Born to nobility
Oya	To beckon
Oz	Strength
Ozzie	God's divine power
Ozzy	God's divine power

P

Pablo	Borrowed
Paco	From the name Francisco
Paddy	From the name Patrick
Padmadhish	Lord Vishnu; Lord of lotus
Padmaj	Lord Brahama
Padmayani	Lord Brahama; Lord Buddha
Padmesh	Lord Vishnu
Padminish	Lord of lotuses; Sun
Page	Youthful assistant
Pahana	Lost white brother
Paisley	Fashion teardrop print
Palani	Free man
Palash	Tree
Paley	From the name Paul

Pallas	Understanding
Pallaton	Fighter
Pallav	Sprouts
Palmer	Palm bearer; Peacemaker
Palti	My escape; Deliverance
Panaki	Lord Vishnu; Son of fire
Pananaj	Lord Hanuman; Son of the God
Panav	Prince
Panavim	One who has a small drum
Panchal	Lord Shiva
Pancho	Tuft; Plume
Pankaj	Lotus
Pankajan	Lotus; Lord Vishnu
Pannagesh	Lord Shiva; The Lord of the serpents
Panshul	Lord Shiva
Paolo	Small
Parag	Famous
Param	Ultimate
Paranjay	Lord of the sea
Paras	Touchstone
Parashar	A renowned saint
Paresh	Lord Brahma
Parikshit	Proven
Parimal	Fragrance

Paris	City in France
Paritosh	Delight
Park	Cypress tree
Parker	Park keeper
Parkin	Young Peter
Parley	To speak
Parmeet	Wisdom
Parmesh	Lord Vishnu
Parrish	Neighbourhood
Parry	Son of Harry
Parson	Minister; Clergy
Parth	King; Arjun
Parthiv	Prince of the Earth
Parvesh	Lord of celebrations
Pascal	Easter child; Lamb
Pascha	To pass over; Born on the Easter
Pasha	To pass over; Born on the Easter
Pashupati	Lord Shiva's incarnation
Pat	Of noble descent
Patch	Form of Peter
Patrick	Nobleman
Paul	Small
Paulo	Place of rest
Paulos	Form of Paul

Pavan	Breeze
Pavanaj	Lord Hanuman
Pavel	Little
Pax	Peace
Paxton	Town of peace
Paytah	Fire
Payton	Village of the warrior
Paz	Peace or gold
Pedro	A rock
Peers	A rock
Pekelo	Stone
Pelham	Town of fur skin
Pello	Stone
Pembroke	A broken hill
Penha	Beloved
Penn	Corral
Pepin	Determined
Percival	Piercing the valley
Percy	Piercing the valley
Peregrine	Wanderer
Perrin	Traveller
Perry	Rock
Pete	Rock
Peter	Rock

Peyton	Village of the warrior
Phil	Lover of horses
Philander	Love
Pinakin	Lord Shiva
Pitambar	Lord Vishnu
Piyush	Amrit; Nectar; Sweet water
Prabhakar	Sun
Prabhav	Effect
Prabhu	God
Prachet	Lord Varun
Pradeep	Lamp
Pradhi	Intelligent
Pradyumna	God of love
Prafull	Playful; In bloom
Prahalad	Bliss
Prajesh	Lord Brahma
Prajit	Winning
Prajval	Brightness
Prajvala	Flame
Prakash	Light
Praket	Intelligence
Prakhar	Shape; Summit
Prakrit	Nature; Handsome
Prakruth	Nature

Pramod	Joy
Pramodan	Lord Vishnu
Pran	Life; Force
Pranad	Lord Vishnu; Lord Brahma
Pranav	Symbol
Pranay	Love
Pranesh	Lord of life
Pranjivan	Life
Prasad	Devotional offering
Prasenjit	A King in the epics
Prashant	Cool; Peaceful
Prashray	Love; Respect
Pratap	Glory
Prathmesh	Lord Ganesha
Prathyusha	Sunrise
Pratyus	Before morning
Pravin	Expert; Skilled
Prem	Love
Pretvan	Moving along
Prineet	Content; Satisfied
Prinita	Pleased
Pritam	Lover; Darling; Loved one
Pritesh	Lord of love

Prithish	Lord of the world
Prithvi	Earth
Priyesh	Loved by the God
Pruthivi	Earth
Pulkit	Happy; Thrilled; Overjoyed
Punit	Holy
Purahan	Lord Shiva
Purajit	Lord Shiva
Purandar	Lord Indra
Purayitri	Vishnu; Lord Shiva; Wish granter
Purshottam	Lord Vishnu
Puru	Heaven
Puruhut	Lord Indra; Invoked by many
Pushkal	Lord Shiva
Pushpesh	Lord of flowers

R

Raahi	Traveller
Raanan	Fresh; New
Rabia	Spring
Race	Running competition
Rach	Frog
Rad	Advisor

Radhesh	Lord Krishna
Radhey	Karna
Radley	Red meadow
Radwan	Delight
Rafael	From the name Raphael
Rafe	Form of Ralph
Rafer	Wealthy
Raffaello	Basis for name Raphael
Rafferty	Wealthy
Rafi	Exalted
Rafiki	Friend
Raghav	Lord Ram
Raghnall	Wise and powerful
Raghubir	Lord Rama
Raghuveer	Lord Rama
Raheem	Compassionate
Rahul	Capable
Raimi	Compassionate
Raine	Wise ruler
Rainer	Advisor
Raj	Kingdom
Raja	King
Rajan	King
Rajat	Courage

Rajdeep	The best of kings
Rajeev	Lotus
Rajender	Lord of kings; Emperor
Rajendra	King of gods; Lord Indra
Rajesh	King
Rajinder	Spontaneous
Rajit	Brilliant
Rakshan	Lord Vishnu
Raleigh	Field of birds
Ralph	Wolf counsellor
Ram	Godlike
Ram	Lord Vishnu
Ramadeep	Lord Rama
Ramakanta	Beloved of Ram
Rami	Sniper
Ramiro	Supreme judge
Ramon	From the name Raymond
Ramses	Sun born
Ranae	Resurrected
Ranajay	Victorious
Rance	Short for Laurence
Randall	From the name Ralph
Randeep	The hero of the battle
Randi	Wolf shield

Randolph	Wolf with a shield
Randy	From the name Randolph
Ranger	Forest Protector
Rangle	Cowboy
Rangsey	Seven colours
Ranjiv	Victorious
Raphael	God has healed
Rasbihari	Lord Krishna
Ratan	Gem
Ratish	Lord of love
Ratnabhu	Lord Vishnu
Ratnanidhi	Lord Vishnu
Ratnesh	Lord of jewels; Diamond
Ratul	Truth seeking; Interested
Raul	Wolf counsellor
Ravi	Sun
Ravi	Sun
Ravisharan	Surrender
Ray	Wise protector
Rayirth	Lord Brahma
Raymond	Wise protection
Read	Red-haired
Reagan	Son of the small ruler
Reda	Satisfied

Redell	Red meadow
Redford	Over the red river
Reece	Stream
Reed	A reed or red haired
Reegan	One who rules
Reese	Enthusiastic
Reeves	Steward
Regan	King's heir
Reggie	Advisor to the king
Reginald	Advisor to the king
Regis	Rules
Reid	Red headed
Reidar	Warrior
Reilly	A small stream
Remedy	Cure
Remi	From Reims
Remington	Town of the raven
Remy	From Reims
Ren	Arranger
Renate	Reborn
Rendor	Police officer
Rene	Reborn
Renesh	Lord of love
Renjith	Victory

Renny	Compact strength
Reth	King
Reuben	Behold; A Son
Revelin	Form of Roland
Rex	King
Rey	King
Reynard	Fox
Reynold	King's advisor
Rhett	A stream
Rhodes	Field of roses
Rhys	A stream
Ricardo	From the name Richard
Rich	Powerful; Rich ruler
Richard	Powerful; Rich ruler
Rick	Powerful; Rich
Rico	Strong ruler
Rida	Accept and obey
Rider	Farmer
Rigg	Lives near the ridge
Riley	A small stream
Rin	Park
Ringo	Apple
Rio	River
Riordan	Royal poet

Rishabh	Superior
Rishi	A sage
Rishvanjas	Lord Indra
Ritesh	Lord of truth
Rithwik	Saint
River	From the river
Rob	From the name Robert
Robbin	Famous brilliance
Robert	Bright fame
Robin	Famous brilliance
Rocco	Rest
Rocio	Dewdrops
Rock	A rock
Rockwell	From the rocky spring
Rocky	From the rocks
Rod	Land near the water
Rodd	From the name Rodney
Roddy	From the name Rodney
Roden	Red valley
Roderick	Famous ruler
Rodney	Land near the water
Roger	Fame spear
Rohan	Sandalwood
Rohan	Ascending; Developing bud

Rohinish	Moon
Roho	Soul
Roland	Famed throughout the land
Rollo	Famous in the land
Roman	Of Rome
Romeo	Of the Romans
Romir	Interesting
Romney	Winding river
Ron	Advisor to the king
Ronald	Advisor to the king
Ronan	Little seal
Rong	Glory
Ronnie	From the name Veronica
Ronny	True image
Roosevelt	Field of rose
Roshan	Illumination
Rukminesh	Lord Krishna
Rupang	Beautiful
Rupesh	Lord of the form
Rushabh	Decoration
Rushil	Charming
Rustam	Large; Very tall
Rutva	Speech

S

Saanjh	Evening
Saatatya	Never ending
Sabrang	Rainbow
Sachchit	Lord Brahma
Sachet	Consciousness
Sachh	The truth
Sachish	Lord Indra
Sachish	Lord Indra
Sadabindu	Lord Vishnu
Sadanand	Lord Shiva
Sadashiv	Pure
Sadru	Lord Vishnu
Sagan	Lord Shiva
Sagar	Sea
Sahara	Lord Shiva
Sahasrad	Lord Shiva
Sahishnu	Lord Vishnu
Sai	Flower; Everywhere
Sairam	Lord Sai Baba
Sakaleshwar	Lord of everything
Sakshum	Skillful

Samabashiv	Lord Shiva
Samajas	Lord Shiva
Samanyu	Lord Shiva
Samarjit	Lord Vishnu
Samarth	Lord Krishna
Samavart	Lord Vishnu
Samdarshi	Lord Krishna
Samendu	Lord Vishnu
Samesh	Lord of equality
Sanat	Lord Brahma
Sanchay	Collection
Sandeep	Glowing
Sandesh	Message
Sanhata	Conciseness
Sanjay	Victorious
Sanjit	Who is always victorious
Sanjit	Victorious
Sanjiv	Vital
Sanjoy	Victory
Sanket	Signal
Sannath	Accompanied by a protector
Sannigdh	Always ready
Sanshray	Aim

Santosh	Satisfaction
Sanwariya	Lord Krishna
Saprathas	Lord Vishnu
Saptajit	Conqueror of 7 elements
Saptanshu	Fire
Sarang	Musical instrument; Sun God
Saras	Moon
Sarasi	Lake
Saravana	Clump of reeds
Sargam	Musical notes
Sarish	Equal
Sarojin	Lord Brahma
Sarva	Lord Krishna; Lord Shiva
Sarva	Lord Krishna; Lord Shiva
Sarvad	Lord Shiva
Sarvadev	Lord Shiva
Sarvadharin	Lord Shiva
Sarvag	Lord Shiva
Sarvak	Whole
Sarvambh	Lord Ganesh
Sarvang	Lord Shiva
Sarvashay	Lord Shiva
Sarvavas	Lord Shiva
Sarvendra	God of all

Sarvesh	God of all
Sashwat	Eternal
Sasmit	Ever smiling
Sasta	One who rules
Satadev	God
Satamanyu	Lord Indra
Satanand	Lord Vishnu
Satesh	Lord of hundreds
Sathi	Partner
Satinath	Lord Shiva
Satindra	Lord Shiva
Satish	Lord Shiva
Satkartar	Lord Vishnu
Satpal	Protector
Satpati	Lord Indra
Satvat	Lord Krishna
Satveer	Lord Vishnu
Satvik	Virtuous
Satvinder	Lord of virtue
Satyadev	Lord of truth
Satyajit	Victory of truth
Satyajit	Conquering by truth
Satyam	Honesty
Satyanarayan	Lord Vishnu

Satyendra	Best among truthful
Saumya	Handsome
Saurabh	Fragrant
Saurav	Melodious
Savya	Lord Vishnu
Setu	Sacred symbol
Shaant	Peace and calm
Shailendra	Lord Shiva
Shailesh	Lord of the mountain
Shakti	Power
Shalang	Emperor
Shaligram	Lord Vishnu
Shalina	Courteous
Shalmali	Lord Vishnu's power
Shamak	Makes peace
Shamakarn	Lord Shiva
Shanay	Power of Lord Shani
Shankarshan	Lord Krishna's brother
Shankdhar	Lord Krishna
Shankhapani	Lord Vishnu
Shankhin	Lord Vishnu
Shantanav	Bhishma Pitamaha
Shantanu	Whole
Shantidev	Lord of peace

Shantinath	Lord of peace
Sharabh	Lord Vishnu
Sharad	Autumn
Shashank	Moon
Shashi	Moon
Shauchin	Pure
Shauri	Lord Vishnu
Shekhar	Ultimate; Peak
Shesanand	Lord Vishnu
Shibhya	Lord Shiva
Shighra	Lord Shiva; Lord Vishnu
Shikhandin	Lord Shiva; Lord Vishnu
Shilang	Virtuous
Shilish	Lord of mountains
Shinjan	Music of anklet
Shipirist	Lord Vishnu
Shishir	Winter
Shishul	Baby
Shitikanth	Lord Shiva
Shitiz	Horizon
Shivadev	Lord of prosperity
Shivam	Auspicious; Lord Shiva
Shivanath	Lord Shiva
Shivank	Mark of the Lord

Shivas	Lord Shiva
Shivasunu	Lord Ganesha
Shiven	Lord Shiva
Shivendra	Lord Shiva; Lord Indra
Shivendu	Moon
Shiveshvar	God of welfare
Shivraj	Lord Shiva
Shivram	Lord Shiva; Lord Ram
Shobhan	Splendid
Shoubhit	Lord Krishna
Shreshta	Lord Vishnu
Shresth	Best of all
Shresthi	Best of all
Shreyas	The best
Shrida	Lord Kuber
Shridhar	Lord Vishnu
Shrigopal	Lord Krishna
Shrihan	Lord Vishnu
Shrihari	Lord Vishnu
Shrikant	Lord Vishnu
Shrikar	Lord Vishnu
Shrikeshav	Lord Krishna
Shriman	Gentleman
Shrimat	Lord Vishnu

Shrimat	Lord Vishnu
Shrimohan	Lord Krishna
Shrinand	Lord Vishnu
Shrinath	Lord Vishnu
Shringesh	Lord of pearls
Shriniketan	Lord Vishnu
Shripadma	Lord Krishna
Shripal	Lord Vishnu
Shripati	Lord Vishnu
Shriram	Lord Rama
Shrirang	Lord Vishnu
Shriranjan	Lord Vishnu
Shrisha	Lord Vishnu
Shritan	Lord Vishnu
Shrivarah	Lord Vishnu
Shrivardhan	Lord Vishnu; Lord Shiva
Shrivas	Lord Vishnu
Shrivatsa	Lord Vishnu
Shubaksh	Lord Shiva
Shubendra	Lord of virtue
Shubh	Fortunate
Shubhaksh	Lord Shiva
Shukla	Lord Shiva; Lord Vishnu

Shulandhar	Lord Shiva
Shulin	Lord Shiva
Shvetanshu	Moon
Shvetavah	Lord Indra
Shyam	Dark; Lord Krishna
Shyamak	Lord Krishna
Shyamal	Lord Krishna
Shyamantak	Lord Krishna
Shyamsunder	Lord Krishna
Sidak	Wish
Siddha	Lord Shiva
Siddhadev	Lord Shiva
Siddhanth	Moral
Siddhesh	Lord of the blessed
Siddheshwar	Lord Shiva
Siddhraj	Lord of perfection
Siddid	Lord Shiva
Sindhu	Lord Vishnu
Sindhunath	Lord of the ocean
Sinhag	Lord Shiva
Sinhvahan	Lord Shiva
Sitanshu	Moon
Snehakant	Lord of love
Somadev	Lord of the moon

Somashekhar	Lord Shiva
Somasindhu	Lord Vishnu
Somesh	Moon
Someshwar	Lord Krishna
Soumava	Moon's light
Sourabh	Fragrance
Sourish	Lord Vishnu
Sparsh	Touch
Sriashwin	A good ending
Sridatta	Given by the God
Stavya	Lord Vishnu
Sthavir	Lord Brahma
Subhang	Lord Shiva
Subhash	Who speaks good words
Subodh	Good lesson
Suchendra	Lord of piousness
Suchit	Person with a sound mind
Sudalai	Village God
Sudama	Lord Krishna's friend
Sudeep	Illumined
Sudhang	Moon
Sudhanshu	Moon
Sudhanvan	Lord Vishnu
Sudhendra	Lord of nectar

Sudhindra	Lord of knowledge
Sudhir	Wise
Sudip	Bright
Sudir	Bright
Suhas	Laughter
Suhrid	Lord Shiva
Suhruda	Good hearted
Sujal	Affectionate
Sujay	Victory
Suka	Wind
Suketu	A Yaksha king
Sukhajat	Lord Shiva
Sukhakar	Lord Rama
Sukhashakt	Lord Shiva
Sukhdev	Lord of happiness
Sukhen	Happy boy
Sukhesh	Lord of happiness
Sukumara	Very tender; Very delicate
Sukumaran	A variation of the name
Sulek	Sun
Sulochna	Beautiful eyes
Sumant	Friendly
Sumatinath	Lord of wisdom
Sumedh	Clever

Sumeet	Friendly
Sumeru	Lord Shiva
Sumukh	Lord Shiva
Sumukh	Lord Shiva
Sunashi	Lord Indra
Sunder	Handsome
Suneet	Lord Shiva; Righteous
Sunil	Lord Krishna
Sunjeev	Making alive
Suparn	Lord Vishnu
Supash	Lord Ganesh
Supratik	Lord Shiva
Supratik	Lord Shiva
Suradhish	Lord Indra
Suradip	Lord Indra
Suragan	Lord Shiva
Surajiv	Lord Vishnu
Surarihan	Lord Shiva
Surbhup	Lord Vishnu
Suren	Lord Indra
Surendra	Lord Indra
Suresh	Lord Shiva; Lord Indra
Suri	Lord Krishna

Surup	Lord Shiva
Surush	Shining
Suryadev	Sun God
Suryanshu	Sunbeam
Suryesh	Sun is God
Susadh	Lord Shiva
Susan	Lord Shiva
Susen	Lord Shiva; Lord Vishnnu
Sushant	Quiet
Sushil	Good charactered man; well mannered
Sushim	Moonstone
Sushrut	A great surgeon of old times
Sutantu	Lord Shiva; Lord Vishnnu
Sutej	Lustre
Sutirth	Lord Shiva
Sutoya	A river
Suvarn	Lord Shiva
Suvarn	Lord Shiva
Suvas	Lord Shiva
Suvidh	Kind
Suvir	Lord Shiva
Suyamun	Lord Vishnu
Suyati	Lord Vishnu
Svamin	Lord Vishnu

Svaminath	Lord Ganesh
Svar	Lord Vishnu
Svaraj	Lord Indra
Svarg	Heaven
Svarna	Lord Ganesh
Svarpati	Lord of sound
Svayambhu	Lord Brahma; Lord Vishnu; Lord Shiva
Svayambhut	Lord Shiva
Swami	Lord
Swarit	Towards heaven
Swastik	Auspicious

T

Taksha	King Bharat's son
Talaketu	Bhishma Pitamaha
Talank	Lord Shiva
Talin	Lord Shiva
Talish	Lord of earth
Tamisraha	Surya
Tamoghna	Lord Vishnu; Lord Shiva
Tanak	Prize
Tanav	Flute

Tanay	Of the family
Tanish	Ambition
Tanunashin	Agni
Tanush	Lord Shiva
Tanvir	Strong
Tapan	Sun
Tapas	Heat
Tapesh	The Holy Trinity
Tapeshwar	Lord Shiva
Taradhish	Lord of the stars
Tarakeshwar	Lord Shiva
Taraknath	Lord Shiva
Taran	Lord Vishnu
Tarang	Wave
Tarendra	Prince of stars
Tarun	Boy
Tathagat	Lord Buddha
Tatya	Lord Shiva
Tavish	Heaven
Tejorupa	Brahma
Teyosh	Varuna
Thakarshi	Lord Krishna
Thavanesh	Lord Shiva
Tirranand	Lord Shiva

Tirthankar	Lord Vishnu
Tirthayaad	Lord Krishna
Tirumala	Seven hills
Tisyaketu	Lord Shiva
Toyesh	Lord of water
Triambak	Lord Shiva
Tridhaman	The Holy Trinity
Tridhatri	Lord Ganesha
Trigya	Lord Buddha
Trijal	Lord Shiva
Trikay	Lord Buddha
Trilokanath	Lord Shiva
Trilokesh	Lord Vishnu
Trimaan	Worshipped in three worlds
Trimurti	The Holy Trinity
Trinabh	Lord Vishnu
Trishulank	Lord Shiva
Trishulin	Lord Shiva
Trivikram	A name of God Vishnu
Tunganath	Lord of the mountains
Tungeshwar	Lord of the mountains
Tungish	Lord Shiva; Lord Vishnu
Turag	A thought

Tushar	Winter
Tusya	Lord Shiva
Tuvidyumna	Lord Indra
Tuvijat	Lord Indra

U

Uchadev	Lord Vishnu
Uchehdev	Vishnu
Udarathi	Lord Vishnu
Udarchis	Lord Shiva
Udarchish	Lord Shiva
Uddhav	Lord Krishna's friend
Uddip	Giving light
Uddiran	Lord Vishnu
Uddirn	Lord Vishnu
Uddish	Lord Shiva
Uddiyan	Flying speed
Uddunath	Lord of stars
Udharthi	Lord Vishnu
Udit	Arisen
Udjith	Lord Vishnu
Udu	Water
Udupati	Lord of stars

Uduraj	Lord of stars
Udyam	Action
Udyan	Garden
Ugresh	Lord Shiva
Ujas	First light
Ujendra	Conqueror
Ujjay	Victorious
Ujval	Splendourous
Ukth	Lord Brahma
Ullas	Light
Ulmuk	Lord Indra
Umakant	Lord Shiva
Umanand	Lord Shiva
Umang	Happiness
Umasuthan	Son of Parvathi (Uma)
Umed	Wish
Umesh	Lord Shiva
Umeshwar	Lord Shiva
Unmesh	Eternal happiness; Joy
Unnabh	Highest
Unnatish	Lord of progress
Upendra	Lord Vishnu
Uppas	Gem
Urav	Excitement

Urjani	Lord of strength
Urmiya	Lord of light
Urugay	Lord Krishna

V

Vaagishwar	Lord Brahma; Master of language
Vachaspati	Lord of speech
Vadish	Lord of the body
Vagindra	Lord of speech
Vagish	Lord Brahma
Vahin	Lord Shiva
Vaijayi	Victor
Vaikartan	Name of Karna
Vaikhan	Lord Vishnu
Vaikunth	Abode of Lord Vishnu
Vainavin	Lord Shiva
Vairaj	Spiritual glory
Vairat	Gem
Vairinchya	Lord Brahma's son
Vairochan	Lord Vishnu's son
Vajasani	Lord Vishnu's son
Vajendra	Lord Indra
Vajradhar	Lord Indra

Vajrahast	Lord Shiva
Vajrin	Lord Indra
Vakrabhuj	Lord Ganesha
Vallabh	Most loved
Valmiki	Saint who wrote Ramayan
Vama	Lord Shiva
Vamadev	Lord Shiva
Vanad	Cloud
Vanadev	Lord of the forest
Vanamalin	Lord Krishna
Vanij	Lord Shiva
Vanraj	King of the forest
Vansh	Coming generation of the father
Vansidhar	Lord Krishna
Varad	God of fire
Varadraj	Lord Vishnu
Varana	Holy river
Vardhan	Lord Shiva
Varesh	Lord Shiva
Vareshvar	Lord Shiva
Varin	Gifts
Varindra	Lord of all
Varip	Varuna; Lord of water
Varish	Lord Vishnu

Variyas	Lord Shiva
Varunesh	Lord of water
Vasant	Season; Spring
Vasav	Lord Indra
Vasavaj	Son of Indra
Vasavi	Son of Indra
Vasudev	Lord Krishna's father
Vasumat	Lord Krishna
Vasupati	Lord Krishna
Vasuroop	Lord Shiva
Vatatmaj	Lord Hanuman
Vatsapal	Lord Krishna
Vatsin	Lord Vishnu
Vayu	Lord Hanuman
Vayujat	Lord Hanuman
Vayunand	Lord Hanuman
Vedamohan	Lord Krishna
Vedang	From the Vedas
Vedant	Hindu philosophy
Vedatman	Lord Vishnu
Vedesh	Lord of Vedas
Velan	Lord Shiva's son
Venavir	Lord Shiva's son
Venkat	Lord Vishnu; Lord Krishna

Venkatesh	Lord Vishnu; Lord Krishna
Viamrsh	Lord Shiva
Vibhav	Lord Shiva; Friend
Vibhavasu	Lord Krishna
Vibhor	Ecstatic
Vibhu	Sun
Vibhumat	Lord Krishna
Vibhusnu	Lord Shiva
Vibhut	Strong
Vibodh	Wise
Vidhatru	Lord Shiva
Vidhesh	Lord Shiva
Vidhu	Lord Vishnu
Vidhyadhar	Full of Knowledge
Vidip	Bright
Vidojas	Lord Indra
Vidvatam	Lord Shiva
Vidyut	Brilliant; Lightening
Vighnajit	Lord Ganesh
Vighnesh	Lord Ganesh
Vignesh	Remover of obstacles
Vigrah	Lord Shiva
Vihaan	Morning; Dawn
Vihang	A bird

Vihari	Lord Krishna
Vijay	Victory
Vijayant	Lord Indra
Vijayarathna	Significant among victorious
Vijayendra	God of the victory
Vijayesh	Lord Shiva
Vijender	God of the bravery
Vijval	Intelligent
Vikarnan	Son of Dhritrashtra
Vikas	Progress
Vikern	Errorless
Vikram	Lord Shiva; Record
Vikramin	Lord Vishnu
Vikrant	Brave
Viksar	Lord Vishnu
Vikunth	Lord Vishnu
Vilas	Coolness
Vilohit	Lord Shiva
Vimal	Clean
Vimridh	Lord Indra
Vinahast	Lord Shiva
Vinay	Humility
Vinayak	Lord Ganesh

Vineet	Knowledgeable
Vinesh	Godly
Vinochan	Lord Shiva
Vinod	Pleasant
Vipaschit	Lord Buddha
Vipin	Forest
Vipul	Abundant
Virabhadra	Lord Shiva
Viraj	Sun
Viral	Precious
Viranath	Lord of the brave
Virat	Massive
Virbhanu	Very strong
Virendra	Lord of the heroes
Viresh	Lord Shiva
Vireshvar	Lord Shiva
Virikvas	Lord Indra
Virinchi	Lord Brahma
Virochan	Lord Vishnu
Virurch	The Holy Trinity
Vishakh	Lord Shiva

Y

Yadav	Lord Krishna

Yadavendra	Lord Krishna
Yadunandan	Lord Krishna
Yadunath	Lord Krishna
Yaduraj	Lord Krishna
Yaduvir	Lord Krishna
Yagna	Ceremonial rites to the God
Yaj	A sage
Yajat	Lord Shiva
Yajnadhar	Lord Vishnu
Yajnarup	Lord Krishna
Yajnesh	Lord Vishnu
Yamahil	Lord Vishnu
Yamajit	Lord Shiva
Yamir	Moon
Yash	Success; Goodwill
Yashas	Fame
Yashodev	Lord of fame
Yashpal	Lord of fame
Yathavan	Lord Vishnu
Yatin	Devotee
Yatindra	Lord Indra
Yatish	Lord of devotees
Yayin	Lord Shiva

Baby Names Girls

A

Aabha	Light
Aadarshini	Idealistic
Aadhya	First Power
Aadi	Beginning
Aadita	From the beginning
Aadrika	Mountain
Aakaanksha	Wish or desire
Aakriti	Shape
Aaliyah	Ascender
Aanandita	Purveyor of joy
Aanchal	Shelter
Aaralyn	With song
Aarini	Adventurous
Aarna	Laxmi
Aarohi	A music tune
Aarti	Form of worship

Aarushi	First rays
Aastha	Faith
Aatmaja	Daughter
Aayushi	One with long life
Abba	Born on Thursday
Abbie	Father of Joy
Abby	God is Joy
Abeni	Girl prayed for
Abhilasha	Wish; Desire
Abhirami	Goddess Parvati
Abhiruchi	Beautiful
Aboli	A flower
Abra	Mother of many
Abrianna	Mother of many nations
Abrienda	Opening
Abril	April
Acacia	Thorny
Accalia	Mythical Greek name
Achla	Constant
Ada	Noble; Kind
Adair	Noble; Exalted
Adalia	God is my refuge; Noble
Adamina	The Earth
Adamma	Beautiful girl

Adara	Chaste one
Addison	Son of Adam
Addo	King of the road
Adela	Noble and serene
Adelaide	Noble; Kind
Adele	Noble; Kind
Adelie	Noble meadow
Adita	From the beginning
Aditi	Mother of the Gods
Adiya	God's treasure
Advika	Unique
Adwitiya	Matchless
Agamya	Knowledge; Wisdom
Agrima	Always on the fore front
Ahanti	Gift
Ahilya	Wife of a rishi
Aishi	God's gift
Aishwarya	Wealth; Prosperity
Ajeya	Lord Vishnu
Ajinder	Victories on indries
Ajita	A winner
Akashleena	Star
Akhila	Complete
Akriti	Shape; Form
Akshadha	God's blessings

Akshainie	Goddess Parvati
Akshara	Letter
Akshata	Rice
Akshi	Existence
Akshita	Wonder girl
Alaknanda	A river
Alaknanda	River name
Alankrita	Decorated lady
Alekhya	Which cannot be written
Alisha	Protected
Alka	Beauty
Aloki	Brightness
Alpa	Small
Alpana	Beautiful
Amartya	Immortal; Divine; A God
Amba	Goddess Durga
Ambika	Goddess Parvati
Ambuja	Goddess Lakshmi
Amisha	Beautiful
Amishi	Pure
Amita	Limitless
Amithi	Unique
Amitjyoti	Ever bright
Amodini	Pleasureable

Amolika	Priceless
Amrapali	Disciple of Buddha
Amritambu	Moon
Amukta	Can't be touched; Precious
Amvi	A Goddess
Anagha	Without sin
Anagi	Valuable
Anahita	Full of grace
Anamika	Without a name
Anamitra	The Sun
Anandani	Joyful
Anandi	Joyful; Unending
Ananti	Gift
Anarghya	Priceless
Anchal	Shelter
Angarika	Flower
Angha	Beauty
Angoori	Grape
Anika	Goddess Durga
Anjali	Tribute
Anjana	Mother of Lord Hanuman
Anjika	Blessed
Anjini	Mother of Lord Hanuman
Anju	Blessings; Inconquerable

Ankita	Emperess; Conqueress
Ankolika	An embrace
Anmol	Priceless
Annada	Goddess Durga
Annapoorna	Goddess of grains
Annika	Goddess Durga
Anokhi	Different
Anouka	Spirit of God
Ansha	Portion
Anshi	God's gift
Anshika	Minute particle
Anshita	A part of
Anshu	Sun
Anshula	Sunny
Anshumali	Sun
Ansuya	Learned woman
Antara	Beauty
Antariksha	Space; Sky
Anubhuti	Feelings
Anudeepthi	Divine light
Anugraha	Divine blessing
Anuhya	Little sister
Anuja	Younger sister
Anukampa	God's grace

Anukeertana	Praising God's virtues
Anukriti	Photograph
Anula	Not wild; Agreeable
Anulekha	Beautiful picture
Anupama	Beautiful
Anuprabha	Followed by glory
Anupriya	Beloved daughter
Anuradha	Lord Krishna's consort
Anusha	Following desires
Anvi	One of Devi's names
Anvita	One who bridges the gap
Anwesha	Quest
Anwita	Goddess Durga
Aparajita	Undefeated
Aparjita	Never been conquered
Aparna	Goddess Parvati
Apeksha	Desire
Apekshaa	Expectation
Apinaya	Expressions in dance
Apurba	Never seen before
Apurva	Like never before
Aradhana	Prayer
Archana	Worship

Arij	Sweet smell
Arkita	Plentiful
Armita	Desire
Arpana	Offering
Arpita	Dedication
Arti	Prayer Ceremony
Aruna	Sun
Arundhati	Fidelity; The morning star
Arunima	Glow of dawn
Aryahi	Goddess Durga
Aryana	Of noble birth/family
Ashika	Person without sorrow
Ashima	Limitless
Ashita	River Yamuna
Ashlesha	A star
Ashwabha	Lightening
Ashwini	Name of the star
Asmita	Pride
Atmikha	Light of the God
Atreyi	A river
Atula	Uncomparable
Avaapya	Achieving
Avanish	Lord of the Earth
Avanti	Modest

Avighna	Ignorant
Avinashi	Indestructable
Avinashika	Indestructable
Avni	The Earth
Avnita	The Earth

B

Babita	Little girl
Bhagirathi	The Ganges
Bhagwanti	Lucky
Bhagwati	Goddess Durga
Bhagyashri	Goddess Lakshmi; Lucky
Bhagyawati	Lucky
Bhakti	Prayer
Bhamini	Lady
Bhanu	Sun; fame
Bhanumati	Famous
Bhanuni	Charming woman
Bhanupriya	The Sun's beloved
Bhanusri	Rays of Laxmidevi
Bharati	Goddess Saraswati
Bharavi	Radiant Sun
Bhaumi	Goddess Sita
Bhavana	Feeling

Bhavani	Goddess Parvati
Bhavi	Emotional
Bhavika	Cheerful expression
Bhavini	Emotional
Bhavishya	Future
Bhavna	Good Feelings; Emotions
Bhawna	Feelings
Bhumika	Earth
Bhuvana	Goddess of the Earth
Bhuvi	Heaven
Bijal	Lightening
Bijli	Lightening
Bina	Melodious
Bindhiya	Dew drop
Bindu	Point
Binita	Modest
Bipasha	River
Bishakha	Star
Bona	Good
Bonita	Pretty; Beautiful
Bonnie	Pretty girl
Bozica	Born at Christmas
Bracha	A blessing
Brady	Broad shouldered

Braima	Father of multitudes
Braith	Freckled
Brandi	Warm and comforting
Brandie	Sweet Nectar
Brandy	Warm and comforting
Branxton	Unknown
Brasen	God's gift
Brayden	Brave
Brazil	Strife
Brinda	Radha
Brishti	Rain
Bulbul	Nightingale

C

Calixte	Very beautiful
Calla	Beauty
Callia	Beautiful
Callie	Beautiful
Calliope	One with beautiful voice
Callista	Most beautiful
Calvine	Bald
Cam	From the name cameron
Cambree	From Wales

Cambria	From Wales
Camdyn	Winding Valley
Cameo	Shadow Portrait
Cameron	Bent Nose
Camila	Attendant
Camilla	Young; Virginal
Camryn	Bent Nose
Cana	Beloved
Candace	Fire White; Pure
Candice	Fire White
Candid	Hidden
Candida	Pure; bright
Candide	Pure; bright
Candie	Bright; Sweet
Candra	Pure and chaste
Candy	Bright; Sweet
Caolan	Form of Helen
Caprice	Fanciful
Capricorn	The Goat
Capucine	Hood
Cara	Dearest
Caraf	Love
Caresse	Beloved
Carey	Pure

Carina	Dear One
Carissa	Beloved
Carla	Strong One
Carlin	Little champion
Carlotta	Strong One
Carly	Strong One
Carlyn	Small and womanly
Carlynda	Strong and beautiful
Carman	Lord of the castle
Carmela	Garden
Carmen	Song
Carminda	Beautiful song
Chaitna	Sunflower seed
Chakori	Alert
Chalama	Goddess Parvati
Chaman	Garden
Chameli	A flower
Chanchal	Active
Chandan	Sandalwood
Chandana	Sandal
Chandani	Moon light
Chandi	Great Goddess
Chandika	Goddess Durga
Chandni	Moon light

Chandra	Moon
Chandralekha	Ray of the moon
Chandramouli	Lord Shiva
Chandrima	Moon
Charu	Beautiful
Charulata	Creeper
Charusheela	Beautiful jewel
Charusmita	One with a beautiful smile
Charvi	A beautiful lady
Chatri	Umbrella
Cheshta	To try
Chetna	Power of intellect; Alert
Chhaaya	Shadow
Chhavi	Reflection
Chhaya	Shadow
Chinmayee	Blissful
Chintanika	Meditation
Chitra	Drawing
Chitrakshi	Colourful eyes
Chitralekha	Portrait

D

Dacey	Down below
Dagan	Grain of corn

Dagmar	Glorious
Dahlia	Flower named after botanist A. Dahl
Dakota	Native American tribal name
Daksha	The Earth; Wife of Lord Shiva
Dakshayani	Goddess Durga
Dalaja	Honey
Danica	Morning Star
Daniela	God is my judge
Danielle	God is my judge
Danika	Morning star
Danna	To give a gift
Daphne	Laurel tree
Dara	Compassionate
Daray	Dark
Darby	Free man
Darcie	Of the dark
Darcy	Dark one
Darena	Famous and loved
Daria	Affluent; wealthy
Darice	Queenly
Darla	Dear; Loved one
Darlita	Young girl
Darpana	Mirror
Darshana	Observation

Darva	Honey bee
Daryl	Dear; Beloved
Dasha	Gift of the God
Datherine	Beloved virgin
Dava	Beloved
Daveigh	Beloved
Davin	Finnish person
Davina	Beloved
Daw	Stars
Dawn	Diana; Sunrise
Da-xia	Big Hero
Day	Light and hope
Daya	Compassion
Dayamayi	Merciful
Dayanita	Merciful
Dayita	Beloved
Dayton	Bright and sunny town
Dea	Goddess
Deana	As Dina - God has judged
Deanna	Divine; Valley
Deanne	Divine
Deborah	Honey Bee
Decima	The Tenth
Dee	Initial D

Deena	Valley (from Dinah)
Deepa	Light
Deepal	Light
Deepika	Lamp; Light
Deepjyoti	The light of the lamp
Deepshika	Lamp
Deepti	Full of Light
Deiondre	Valley
Deirdra	Sorrowful; Wanderer
Deka	Pleasing
Delaney	Enemy's child
Delfina	Dolphin
Delila	Hair or Poor
Delilah	Night
Della	Of the Nobility
Delling	Scintillating
Delphina	Little flower
Delta	Mouth of a river
Delu	The only girl
Demeter	Lover of the Earth
Demetra	Goddess of Fertility
Demetria	Goddess of Fertility
Demi	Half; Small
Demira	Devotee of Lord Krishna

Dena	Valley or vindicated
Denali	Great One
Desna	Offering
Devangi	Like a Goddess
Devanshi	Divine
Devapriya	Dear to the Gods
Devashree	Goddess Lakshmi
Deveshi	Goddess Durga
Devi	Goddess
Devika	Goddess
Devina	Like a Goddess
Devkanya	Divine damsel
Devki	Lord Krishna's mother
Devna	Godly
Dhanvanti	Holding wealth
Dhanvi	Money
Dhanya	Thankful; Lucky
Dhara	Earth; Flow
Dharini	Earth
Dharitri	The Earth
Dharmini	Religious
Dharmista	Lord in dharma
Dharti	Earth
Dharuna	Supporting

Dheeptha	Goddess Lakshmi
Dhriti	Patience
Dhruti	Motion
Dhruvi	Firm
Dhruvika	Firmly fixed
Dhuha	Forenoon
Dhwani	Melody; Music
Dhyana	Meditation
Diana	Bright one
Diksha	Initiation
Dilan	Son of the sea
Dipali	Lamps
Dipashri	Lamp
Dipti	Brightness
Disha	Direction; Side
Dishi	Direction
Dishita	Focus
Diva	Goddess Singer
Diviya	Divine power
Divya	Divine power
Divyana	Divine
Divyata	Divine lights
Diya	Lamp
Diyajal	Light

Drishti	Sight
Drishya	Sight
Drithi	Patience
Durga	A Goddess
Dyumna	Glorious
Dyuti	Light

E

Eara	From the East
Earlene	Pledge
Easter	From the holiday
Eavan	Fair Ones
Ebony	Dark strength
Echo	Sound returned
Edalene	Noble; King
Edaline	Noble; King
Edana	Tiny flame
Edda	With clear goals
Edeline	Born into Nobility
Eden	Paradise
Edie	Treasure
Edith	Happy
Edna	Spirit renewed

Edolie	Noble; Good
Edwina	Valuable friend
Edythe	Happy
Effie	Melodious talk
Eileen	Light; from Helen
Eilis	Noble; Kind
Eithne	Little fire
Ekaa	Goddess Durga
Ekaja	Only child
Ekani	One
Ekanta	Devoted girl
Ekantika	Solely focussed
Ekta	Unity
Elaine	Light
Elam	Highlands
Elan	Tree
Elani	Light
Elata	Happy
Elda	Old
Ella	She
Elle	Woman; Girl
Ellema	Milking a cow
Ellen	Light
Ellery	Elder tree Island

Ellette	Little elf
Ellie	Light
Elon	God loves me
Elpida	Hope
Elsie	Consecrated to God
Elspeth	Consecrated to God
Elu	Full of grace
Elvira	Impartial judgement
Elwyn	Pale brow
Elysia	The blessed home
Eman	Faith
Emanuele	God in humankind
Ember	Spark; Burning low
Emberlynn	Precious pretty jewel
Emelda	Emerald-like
Emele	Industrious; Admiring
Emera	Industrious leader
Emerald	A bright green gem
Emiko	Blessed; Beautiful child
Emilia	Admiring
Emilie	Ambitious; Industrious
Emily	Admiring
Ereshva	Righteous
Esha	Desire; Want

F

Fabienne	Bean grower
Fabiola	Bean grower
Faith	To trust
Fala	A crow
Falala	Born in abundance
Falguni	Beautiful
Fallon	Of a ruling family
Fanchon	Free; Whimsical
Fancy	Decorated
Fareeda	Unique
Farica	Chief of peace
Farren	Wanderer
Fathia	Victory
Fatima	Daughter of the Prophet
Fauna	Goddess of Fertility
Faunia	Young deer
Faunus	God of forests
Fausta	Fortunate
Faustine	Lucky
Fauve	Wild and uninhibited
Fawn	Young deer

Fawzia	Winner
Fay	Fairy or elf
Faye	Fairy or elf
Fayre	Beautiful
Finola	White haired
Fiona	White; Fair
Fiorella	Little flower
Fiorenza	Flower
Fisseha	Happiness; Joy
Flan	From flannery
Flannery	Flat Land
Fleta	Swift
Flora	Flowering
Floramaria	Flower of Mary
Florence	Prosperous; Flowering
Floria	Flowering
Floriane	Flowering
Florida	Flowering
Fola	Honour
Fonda	The Earth; Grounded
Forest	From the woods
Forever	Never ending
Fountain	A spring
Fran	Free

Frances	Free
Francesca	Free
Fredrica	Peace
Fredricka	Peaceful Ruler
Freira	Sister
French	From France
Frieda	Peace; Joy

G

Gajra	Flowers
Gandhali	Sweet scent
Ganga	Sacred River
Gangika	River
Ganika	Flower
Ganjan	Exceeding
Garima	Warmth
Gauri	Goddess Parvati
Gaurika	Pretty young girl
Gayathri	Phased verse
Gayatri	Goddess Saraswati
Geet	Melody
Geeta	Holy book of the Hindus
Geeti	Melody

Geetika	A small song
Gehna	Ornament
Gina	Silvery
Ginni	Precious gold coin
Giribala	Goddess Parvati
Girisha	Goddess Parvati
Gita	Holy book
Gitali	Melodious
Gitanjali	Melodious tribute
Gitashri	The Bhagvad Gita
Goldy	Made of gold
Gopa	Gautama's wife
Gorma	Goddess Parvati
Gowri	Bright; Goddess Parvati
Granthana	Book
Greashma	Summer
Greeshma	Kind of season
Grishma	Warmth
Gulab	Rose
Gulika	A pearl
Guneet	Full of talent
Gunjan	Humming
Gunnika	Garland
Gurbani	Sikh's religious

prayer

Gurinder	Lord
Gurneet	Guru's Moral
Gurparveen	Goddess of the Stars

H

Hamsa	Swan
Hansa	Swan
Hansuja	Laxmi
Hari priya	Goddess Laxmi
Haribala	Daughter of Lord Vishnu
Harini	A deer
Harita	Green
Harjas	Praise of the God
Harley	Place; Name
Harshi	Joyous
Harshini	Joyful
Harsika	Laugh
Hasita	Full of laughter
Hela	Moonlight
Hema	Gold
Hemadri	Golden hills
Hemakshi	Golden eyes

Hemal	Golden
Hemangi	Golden bodied
Hemani	Goddess Parvati
Hemavati	Goddess Parvati
Hena	Flower
Hera	Queen of Gods
Hetal	Happy
Heti	Sun ray
Hima	Snow
Himaja	Goddess Parvati
Himani	Gowri
Himanshi	Part of snow
Hina	A shrub
Hind	Proper name
Hiral	Wealthy
Hiranmayi	Like a deer
Hitaishi	Well wisher
Hradini	Lightening
Hridya	Heart

I

Idika	The Earth
Iditri	Complimentary

Iksha	Sight
Ikshita	Visible
Ikshula	Holy River
Ila	Vitality
Imani	Trustworthy
Indali	Powerful
Indira	Bestower of wealth
Indrani	Indra's wife
Indu	Moon
Induja	Moon's daughter
Indulekha	Moon
Inu	Attractive
Ipsita	Desire
Ira	Earth; Goddess Saraswati
Iraja	Wind's daughter
Ishana	Goddess Durga
Ishani	Goddess Durga
Ishanvi	Parvati
Ishi	Goddess Durga
Ishita	Superior
Ishwarya	God's prosperity
Ishwarya	Wealth; Prosperity
Ishya	Spring
Itkila	Fragrant

J

Jagravi	King
Jagruti	Awareness
Jagvi	Worldly
Jahan	The World
Jahnavi	River Ganga
Jala	Clarity; Elucidation
Jalpa	Discussion
Jalsa	Celebration
Janani	Name of three Goddesses
Janki	Goddess Sita
Januja	Female offspring
Janya	Life
Jasmin	A flower
Jasminder	Lord's glory
Jasmine	Fragrant flower
Jasmit	Famed
Jasweer	Victorious
Jayan	Victory
Jayanti	Goddess Parvati
Jayashree	Victorious woman
Jayati	Victorious

Jeetesh	Goddess of Victory
Jeevitha	Life
Jharna	A spring
Jigisha	Superior
Jigna	Intellectual curiosity
Jignasa	Academic curiosity
Jilpa	Life giving
Jital	Winner
Jivantika	One who gives life
Joshika	Young maiden
Joshitha	Pleased
Juhi	Flower
Jui	Flower
Jyeshtha	Biggest
Jyothi	Light
Jyothishmathi	Goddess Durga
Jyoti	Light; Brilliant

K

Kaajal	Muscara (surma)
Kaamla	Perfect
Kaasni	Flower
Kadambari	Female cuckoo

Kahkashan	Stars
Kairavi	Moonlight
Kajol	Eye liner
Kajri	Light as a cloud
Kakoli	The preaching of a bird
Kala	Art
Kali	Bud
Kalika	Loud
Kalima	Blackish
Kalini	Flower
Kalpana	Imagination
Kalpita	Imaginary
Kalyani	Fortunate
Kamal	Lotus
Kamala	Goddess Lakshmi
Kamalika	Lotus
Kamalini	Lotus
Kamana	Wish
Kanjri	Bird
Kanta	Beauty
Kanthi	Lustre; Loveliness
Kanti	Light
Kanupriya	Radha
Kapila	Sacred cow

Kareena	Flower
Karishma	Miracle
Karona	Merciful; Forgiving
Karthiaeini	Indian Goddess name
Karuli	Innocent
Karuna	Merciful
Karunya	Compassionate
Kashi	Luminous; Pilgrimage spot
Kashika	The shiny one
Kashvi	Shining
Kashwini	Star
Kashyapi	Earth
Kasturi	Scented
Kaumudi	Full moon
Kaushali	Skillful
Kaushalya	Lord Rama's mother
Kavika	Poetess
Kavita	Poem; Poetry
Kavni	A small poem
Kavya	Poem
Keertana	Song
Keerthana	Devotional song
Kishmish	Dry fruit
Kishori	Young damsel

Kokila	A singer
Komal	Soft
Komali	Tender
Kompal	Bud
Kopal	A Rose Bud
Kosha	Origin; Name of river
Kripi	Beautiful
Krisha	Divine
Krishna	Lord Krishna
Krittika	Name of a star
Krupa	God's forgiveness
Krupali	Who always forgives
Kruthika	Name of a star
Kruti	Creation
Kshama	Flame
Kshama	Forgiveness; Mercy
Kshamya	Earth
Kuhu	The sweet note of the bird
Kuja	Goddess Durga
Kumari	Goddess Durga
Kumkum	Sacred powder (red)
Kumudini	Lotus
Kundan	Gold

Kundanika	Flower
Kunshi	Shining
Kunti	Pandava's mother
Kusum	Flower
Kusumita	Flowers in bloom
Kuvam	Sun
Kuvira	Courageous woman

L

Labuki	Musical instrument
Ladhi	Sangeet
Ladli	Loved one
Lagan	Dedication
Laghuvi	Tender
Lajita	Modest
Lakhi	Goddess Laxmi
Laksha	Aim
Lakshaki	Goddess Sita
Lakshanya	One who achieves
Lakshita	Distinguished
Lakshya	Aim
Lali	Blushing
Lalima	Beauty
Lalita	Beautiful woman

Lamya	Dark-lipped
Lata	Creeper
Latasha	Surprise
Latika	Small creeper
Laura	Laurel
Lavanya	Beauty; Lustre
Laxmi	Goddess of Wealth
Leela	Divine drama
Leena	A devoted one; Tender
Leila	Dark as night
Lekisha	Life
Lemmie	Devoted to the Lord
Likhitha	Writing
Lilavati	God's will
Lipi	Manuscripts of the God
Lipika	Letters; Alphabets
Lochan	Bright eyes
Lola	Goddess Laxmi
Lolita	Ruby
Lopa	Learned

M

Madhavi	Honey

Madhu	Honey
Madhulika	Nectar
Madhumathi	Delight moon
Madhumitha	Sweet person
Madhupriya	Fond of honey
Madhur	Melodious; Sweet
Madhura	Sweet; Pleasant
Madhureema	Honey
Madhuri	Sweet
Madhurima	Sweet girl
Madhusha	Beauty
Madhuvanthi	One who is sweet like honey
Madina	Land of beauty
Magadhi	Flower
Maghi	Giving gifts
Maha	Gazelle
Mahasri	Goddess Laxmi
Mahendi	A paste of leaves
Mahika	Earth
Mahima	Glorious
Mahiya	Joy
Maina	A bird
Maitreyi	A wise woman
Makali	The moon

Malarvizhi	Cute eyes
Malini	Fragrant
Maljumana	Beautiful
Malli	Flower
Malti	Moonlight
Mamta	Motherly love
Mana	Supernatural power
Manaal	Attainment; Achievement
Manali	Bird
Manasi	Mother Goddess
Mandavi	Wife of Bharat
Mandira	Melody
Mani	Gem
Manika	Jewel
Manini	Self respected
Maniratna	Diamond
Manisha	Desire; Wish
Manjari	Bud of a mango tree
Marsha	Respectable
Marta	Lady
Marya	Mark; Limit
Mausam	Season
Mausami	Seasonal
Mawiya	Old Arabic name

Maya	Illusion
Maysaa	To walk with a swinging gait
Mayurakhsi	Eye of the peackock
Mayuri	Pea-hen
Mayurika	Baby pea-hen
Mayyada	To walk with a swinging gait
Medha	Goddess Saraswati; Wisdom; Intellect
Meenakshi	Eye
Megha	Cloud; Rain
Meghavini	Intelligence
Meghna	River Ganges
Meha	Intelligent; Rain
Mehak	Sweet Smell; Aroma Fragrance
Menaja	Goddess Parvati
Mihika	Dew drop
Mikel	Just a name
Milonee	Melodious
Mina	Fish; Jewel
Minakshi	Fish eyes
Minal	Pure
Minu	A gem; Precoius stone
Mira	Cloud
Miraya	Lord Krishna's devotee
Misha	Smile

Mishka	Gift of love
Moksin	Free
Monal	Bird
Monalisa	Noble
Monisha	Intellectual
Moubani	A flower
Mridini	Goddesss Parvati
Mridu	Gentle
Mridula	An ideal woman
Mrinali	Lotus stem
Mrinmayee	Deer's eye
Mrinmoyee	Anything that is made out of mud
Mrittika	Mother Earth
Muna	Wish; Desire
Muneera	Illuminating; Shedding light
Mythri	Beautiful girl

N

Nabanipa	A new flower
Nabhi	Central
Nagina	Jewel
Naila	Acquirer; Obtainer
Naina	Eyes
Nainika	Pupil of the eye

Najla	Of wide eyes
Najwa	Confidential talk; Secret conversation
Najya	Victorious
Namya	Worthy of honour
Nanaki	Sister of Nanak
Nandana	Goddess Durga
Nandi	Goddess Durga
Nandika	Lakshmi
Nandini	Goddess Durga; A delightful Goddess
Nandita	Cheerful
Nandita	One who pleases
Nashita	Energetic and full of life
Naveena	New
Naveta	New
Navika	New
Navistha	Youngest
Navya	Young
Nawal	Gift
Nayonika	One with expressive eyes
Neelam	Blue or dark eyes; Gem
Neelesh	Lord Krishna; The moon
Neelima	Blue sky
Neena	New
Neepa	A flower
Nidhipa	Treasure Lord

Niharika	The girl who is admired by looking at itself
Nikara	Collection
Nikita	Earth; Ganges
Nilshikha	Blue mountain's top
Nilutha	Providing water
Nimisha	Momentary; Minute
Nimita	Fixed
Ninarika	Misty
Nishka	Honest
Nishtha	Determination
Nistha	Firmness
Nithya	Eternal
Niti	Ethics
Nitya	Eternal
Nityasri	With eternal beauty
Nivedita	Offered to the God
Nivedita	Surrendered
Niveditha	Offered to the God
Nivriti	Bliss
Niyati	Destiny
Nona	Ninth
Nudhar	Gold

O

Oditi	Dawn
Ojasvi	Bright
Oma	Life giver
Omisha	Goddess of birth and death
Oorja	The energy
Oparna	Parvati
Orpita	Offering
Oshma	Summer season

P

Padma	Lotus
Padmaja	Goddess Laxmi
Padmashri	Divine Lotus
Padmini	Lotus flower
Padnuni	Lotus
Palak	Eye lid
Palaksi	White
Pari	Fairy
Paridhi	Limit
Parinita	Complete

Parishi	Like a fairy
Parivita	Extermely free
Parmita	Wisdom
Parthavi	Goddess Sita
Parul	Graceful; Flow of water
Parvati	Wife of Lord Shiva
Parvini	Festival
Patala	Goddess Durga
Pauravi	Descendant of Puru
Pavaki	Goddess Saraswati
Pavani	Goddess Ganga
Pavitra	Pure
Payal	Anklets
Pinga	Goddess Durga
Pingla	Goddess Durga
Pooja	Prayer
Poonam	Full moon
Poorna	Complete
Poornakamala	A blooming lotus
Poulomi	Indra's second wife
Prabha	Light
Pracheeta	Origin; Starting point
Prachi	East
Pradnya	Wisdom; Buddhi

Prafula	In bloom
Pragalbha	Goddess Durga
Pragathi	Progress
Pragati	Progress
Pragya	Wisdom
Pramiti	Wisdom
Pranali	Organisation
Pranati	Pranam; Greeting elders with respect
Pranavi	Goddess Parvati
Pranaya	Leader
Praneeta	Led forward; Conducted; Advanced; Promoted
Pranidhi	Spy
Pranita	Promoted
Pranjal	Honest and Dignified
Pranvuta	Praised
Prapti	Advantage
Prarthana	Prayer
Prashanthi	Highest peace
Prasheetha	Origin; Starting point
Prasheila	Ancient time
Prassana	Pleasing; Propitiating
Pratibha	Splendour; Brightness Intelligence
Pratika	Symbolic

Pratima	Idol
Pratitha	Well known
Pratiti	Faith
Pratyusha	Early morning
Praveena	Skilled
Pravesha	To enter
Prayerna	Bhakti; Worship
Prayuta	Mingled with
Preet	Love
Preetha	happy
Preeti	Satisfaction; Happiness
Preksha	Beholding; Viewing
Premila	Full of love
Prerena	Direction; Command
Prerna	Inspiration
Prestha	Dearest
Priyanka	Favourite
Prina	Content
Progya	Prowess
Puji	Gentle
Pujya	Respectable
Pulak	A gem; Smile
Puneet	Pure
Punita	Holy

Punya	Good work
Punya	Virtuous
Purnima	Full Moon
Purva	Elder; Breeze
Purvi	From the east
Pusha	Nourishing
Pushpa	Flower

R

Raaka	Full moon
Rahini	Goddess Saraswati
Rajashri	Royalty
Raji	Shining
Rajika	Lamp
Rajni	Night
Rajrita	Prince of living
Rakhi	Bond of protection
Raksha	Protection
Rakti	Pleasing
Rama	Goddess Laxmi
Ramini	Beautiful woman
Ramita	Pleasing
Ramitha	Pleasing

Ramra	Splendour
Rashmika	A ray of light
Rasna	Ray
Rathna	Pearl
Rati	Joy
Ratti	Wife of Kamdeva
Raveena	Sunny
Revati	Prosperity
Richa	Hymn; The writing of the Vedas
Riddhi	Fortunate
Rishika	Saintly
Rishima	Moonbeam
Rishita	The best
Rita	Way of life
Rithika	Of a stream
Ritika	Movement
Ritika	Of Brass
Ritsika	Traditional
Roopini	Beautiful appearance
Roshni	Light
Rucha	Vedic lyrics
Ruchi	Light
Ruchika	Shining; Beautiful; Desirous
Ruchita	Splendorous

Rudrani	Goddess Parvati
Rugu	Soft
Ruhi	Soul
Ruhin	Spiritual
Rujuta	Polite
Rukan	Steady; Confident
Rukhmini	Goddess Laxmi
Rukma	Gold
Ruma	Vedic hymn
Runa	Sixth month
Rupa	Silver
Rupal	Made of silver
Rupashi	Beautiful
Rupeshwari	Goddess of beauty
Rupika	Gold coin
Rusham	Peaceful
Rushda	Good News
Ruth	Season
Rutuja	Queen of seasons
Rutva	Speech
Ruwayda	Walking gently

S

Saachee	Beloved

Saanjh	Evening
Saanvi	Goddess Lakshmi
Saashi	Moon
Saatvika	Calm
Sabrang	Rainbow
Sabri	Lord Rama's devotee
Sachi	Grace
Sachita	Wise
Sadabhuja	Goddess Durga
Sadgata	Who moves in the right direction
Sadhana	Goddess Durga
Sadhika	Goddess Durga
Sadhna	Worship
Sadvita	Combination
Sagarika	Wave
Sagun	Auspicious
Saloni	Beautiful
Samali	Bouquet
Samapti	Wealth
Samar	Evening conversations
Sameeksha	Abstract
Sanika	Flute
Sanjana	In harmony

Sanjaya	Triumphant
Sanjeevani	Immortality
Sanjita	Triumphant
Sanjna	Well known
Sanjoli	Period of twilight
Sanjukta	Connection; Union
Sanjula	Beautiful
Sanobar	Palm tree
Sanoja	Eternal
Sansita	Praise
Sanskriti	Heritage
Sanskruti	Culture
Santosh	Satisfaction
Santoshi	Goddess name
Santushti	Complete satisfaction
Sanyukta	Relating to union
Sapna	Dream
Saumyaa	Goddess Durga
Saumyi	Moonlight
Saura	Celestial
Savidharani	Sun God
Savita	Sun
Savitha	Bright
Savitri	Mother

Sawda	Proper name
Sawsan	Lily of the valley
Sayantini	Evening
Sayuri	Flower
Seema	Border; Limit
Sharmista	Wife of Yayathi
Sharmistha	Yayathi's (a king) wife
Sharvani	Goddess Durga
Sharvari	Twilight
Shasha	Moon
Shashi	Moon
Shashini	Moon
Shatakshi	Goddess Durga
Shatha	Aromatic
Shaveta	Saraswati
Sheela	Character
Sheetal	Cool
Shefali	Fragrance
Shehla	Dark brown; Almostblack
Shelly	Style; Manne A river
Shibani	Goddess Durga
Shichi	Glow

Shielawatti	River
Shiesta	Modest; Disciplined; Cultured; eminent
Shikha	Hill top
Shila	Rock
Shilpa	Perfectly created
Shipra	River's name
Shireesha	Flower
Shirina	Night
Shiuli	Flower
Shivakanta	Goddess Durga
Shivali	Goddess Parvati
Shravanthi	A name in Buddhist literature
Shravya	Musical tone
Shraya	Perfect
Shreema	Prosperous
Shresta	Foremost; Best; First
Shresthi	Best of all
Shreyasi	One who is most beautiful
Shridevi	Goddess Laxmi; Goddess of wealth
Shridulla	Blessing
Shrika	Fortune
Shrikala	Goddess Laxmi
Shrikama	Radha

Shrila	Beautiful
Shrilaxmi	Goddess Laxmi
Shrilekha	Goddesses Lakshmi & Saraswathi
Shrimayi	Fortunate
Shristhi	Creation; Remembrance
Shrivali	Goddess Laxmi
Shrividya	Goddess Durga
Shriya	Prosperity
Shriyadita	Sun
Shrujana	Creative and intelligent girl
Shrujeshwari	Goddess of creativity
Shrusti	World
Shruthika	Lord Parvati
Shrutika	Not none
Shubha	Lucky for everybody
Shubhangi	Beautiful
Shuchi	Pure
Shulini	Goddess Durga
Shushma	Fragrant
Shutradevi	Goddess Saraswati
Shveni	White
Shveta	White
Shweta	Lovable; White

Shwetha	White
Shwiti	Fairness
Shyama	Goddess Durga
Shyamala	Goddess Durga ;Pond
Simi	Limit
Sivanandhini	Devotee of Lord Shiva
Sivaneswary	God Shiva's name
Smruti	Memory
Sneha	Friendship; Friendly nature; Related to love
Snehal	Love; Bring love to people
Snehelata	Vine of love
Snehi	Friendly
Snigda	Affectionate
Snikitha	Smiling ace
Sobaika	Gold
Sobhonika	Good looking
Sorrila	Tranquil
Sona	Gold
Sonakshi	Goddess Parvati
Sonal	Golden
Sonali	Golden
Soneera	Clean water
Sonia	Pretty Girl; Gold
Sonita	Young Sun

Sougandika	Sacred River
Souganthika	Related to flower; Used for worship
Sowjanya	Tender
Sowmya	Peace
Spandana	Motivation
Srijani	Creativity
Srilatha	Wealth creeper
Srinithi	Goddess Lakshmi
Srirupa	Laxmi's Beauty
Subhashini	Nice girl
Subhasini	Soft-spoken
Subhi	Lucky
Subhiksha	Full-fill
Subiksha	Prosperous
Sucharita	Good character
Sucheta	Always alert
Suchhaya	Shining
Suchismita	With a pious smile
Suchita	Auspicious
Suchitra	Beautiful
Sudarshini	Beautiful lady (sundari)
Sudha	Nectar
Sudhira	Placid

Sudiksha	Goddess Laxmi
Sudipta	Bright
Sugandha	Fragrant
Sugauri	Goddess Parvati
Suggi	Harvest
Suhagi	Lucky
Suhani	Pleasant
Suhas	Laughter
Suhayma	Small arrow
Sujitha	Great conqueror
Sukhmani	Bringing peace to heart
Sukirti	Fame; Well praised
Suman	Flower
Sumedha	Intelligent
Sumita	Friendly
Sumitra	Friendly
Sumona	Calm
Sunaina	Beautiful eyes
Sunanda	Sweet charactered
Sunayana	A woman with lovely eyes
Sunayna	Beautiful eyes
Sundara	Beautiful; Charming; Noble
Sundari	Beautiful
Sunhari	Golden

Suniska	With beautiful smile
Sunita	Well-behaved
Suparna	Goddess Parvati
Supreetha	Beloved; Endearing to all
Suprema	Loving
Suprit	Loving
Supriya	Well-loved
Surabhi	Beauty
Surangi	Colourful
Surasa	Goddess Durga
Surasti	Perfect
Svadhi	Thoughtful
Svaha	Wife of fire god
Svana	Sound
Svara	Goddess of sound
Svitra	White
Swapanthi	Goddess Lakshmi
Swapna	Dream like
Swapnika	Dream
Swara	Tones or self-shining in Sanskrit
Swarna	Gold
Swarnika	Gold
Swati	Star

T

Talika	A bird
Talli	Young
Tamadhur	Proper name
Tanaya	Daughter
Tanirika	Flower
Tanisha	Ambition
Tanisi	Goddess Durga
Tanmaya	Reincarnated
Tanmayee	Ecstasy (in Sanskrit & Telugu)
Tansi	Beautiful Princess
Tanu	Slim
Tanuja	Born of the body; Daughter
Tarita	Goddess Durga
Tarjni	Third finger
Tarla	Nectar
Tarli	Star
Taroob	Merry
Taru	Small Plant
Taruna	Young girl
Taruni	Young girl
Tejasvi	Energetic; Gifted; Brilliant

Teta	Innocent Beauty
Thanaa	Thankfulness
Triambika	Goddess Parvati
Tridiva	Heaven
Trijagati	Goddess Parvati
Trilochana	Goddess Parvati
Tripta	Satisfaction
Tripti	Satisfaction
Tripura	Goddess Durga
Triputa	Goddess Durga
Trisha	Wish; Desire
Trishala	Trident
Trishna	Desire
Trishona	Desire
Trishulini	Goddess Durga
Triti	A moment in time
Triya	Young girl
Turvi	Superior
Turya	Spiritual power
Tvadeeya	Belongs to Lord
Tvarita	Goddess Durga

U

Ubika	Growth

Ucchal	Perception
Udantika	Satisfaction
Udgita	A hymn
Udipti	On fire
Udita	Risen
Udyati	Elevated
Ujhala	Light
Ujvala	Bright; Lighted
Unma	Joy
Unnathi	Progress
Unnati	Progress
Unni	Lead
Upadhriti	A ray
Upasana	Worship
Upasna	Worship
Upkar	Gift
Upma	The best
Urvashi	The Ganges
Urvi	Earth
Usha	Dawn
Usharvi	Raga in the morning
Ushi	A plant
Usra	First light
Utalika	Wave
Utkarsha	Proud

V

Vaagdevi	Goddess of learning; Goddess Saraswati
Vagishwari	Goddess Saraswati
Vaibhavi	Affluence
Vaidarbhi	Rukhmini; Wife of Krishna
Vaidehi	Sita; Wife of Ram
Vamsi	Flute of Lord Krishna
Vanaja	Lotus
Vanalika	Sunflower
Vandana	Adoration
Vanishri	Goddess Saraswati
Vanita	Graceful lady
Vanmalli	Wild flower
Vanmayi	Goddess Saraswati
Vanshi	Flute
Vanshika	Flute
Vara	Blessing
Varaa	Goddess Parvati
Varali	Moon
Varalika	Goddess Durga
Varshana	Birth place of Radha

Vijayanthi	Winning
Vimudha	Goddess Lakshmi
Vinutha	Exceptionally new
Vivekka	Intelligent and witty
Vividha	Strange
Vritee	Nature; Behaviour

Y

Yachana	Pleading
Yadavi	Goddess Durga
Yahvi	Heaven; Earth
Yashita	Successful
Yashna	One with fame
Yashoda	Foster mother of Lord Krishna
Yashodhara	Glory
Yashvi	Fame
Yayaati	Wanderer; Traveller
Yesha	Fame
Yochana	Thought
Yoga	An art of achieving happiness
Yogita	A female disciple

Goodwill's All About Series

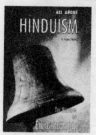

All About

How to improve

grammar

Hone Your Grammatical Skills

ALL ABOUT

How to improve your

Select the right word

CAVE
BOAT
STENCIL
RACE
BABY
PLUM
PULL
PLAIN
DRAW
CLAY

ALL ABOUT

Hypnotism

ALL ABOUT

ISLAM

The Religion of Monotheism

ALL ABOUT

the secret of

magic

Learn to Bewitch

ALL ABOUT

MAGNETOTHERAPY

the Healing

Currents

ALL ABOUT

Marketing
Techniques

Be on Target

ALL ABOUT

Meditation

the

Relaxation

ALL ABOUT

Increasing

Memory Power

Sharpen your Brain

ALL ABOUT

Self

Motivation

Spin the web of inspiration

ALL ABOUT

Nostrodamus

ALL ABOUT

Nutrition

ALL ABOUT

Personality
Development

Become a
Better
Person

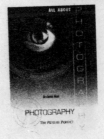

ALL ABOUT

PHOTOGRAPHY

PHOTOGRAPHY

ALL ABOUT

Reiki